Contents

This book belongs to

Say the Sounds

Look Out
For Me

snail

toad

pup

sheep

fox

butterfly

Star
and Fish

star

fish

starfish

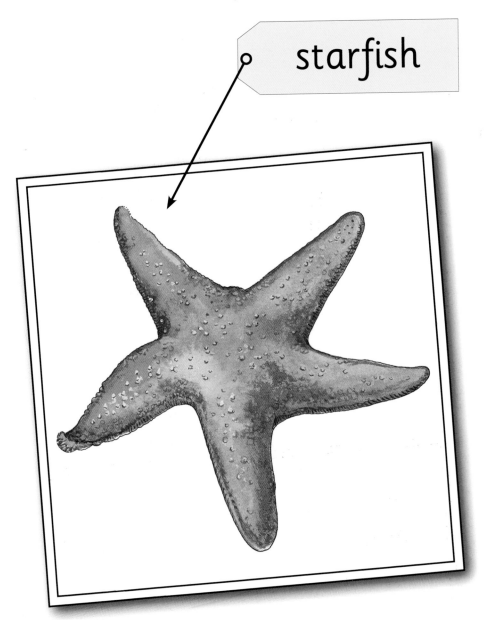

tooth

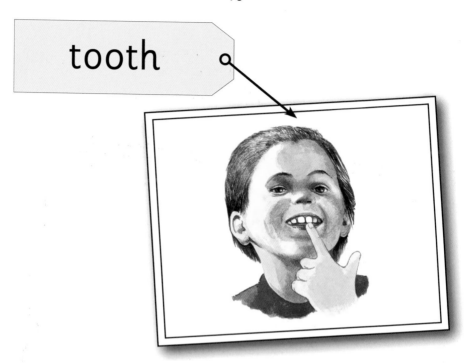

brush

toothbrush

toad

stool

toadstool

lip

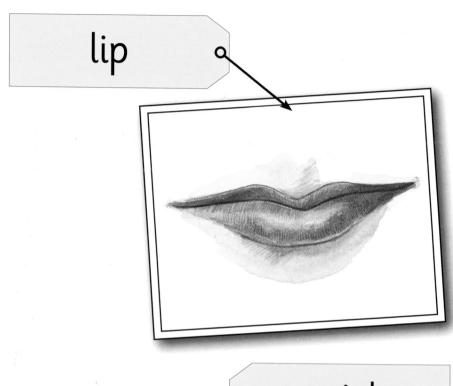

stick

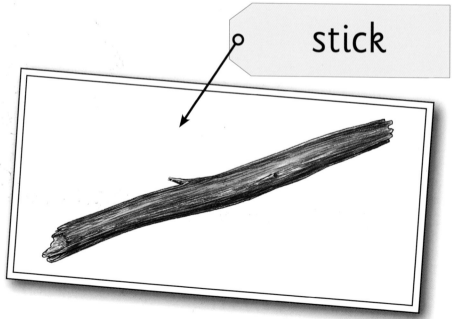

lipstick

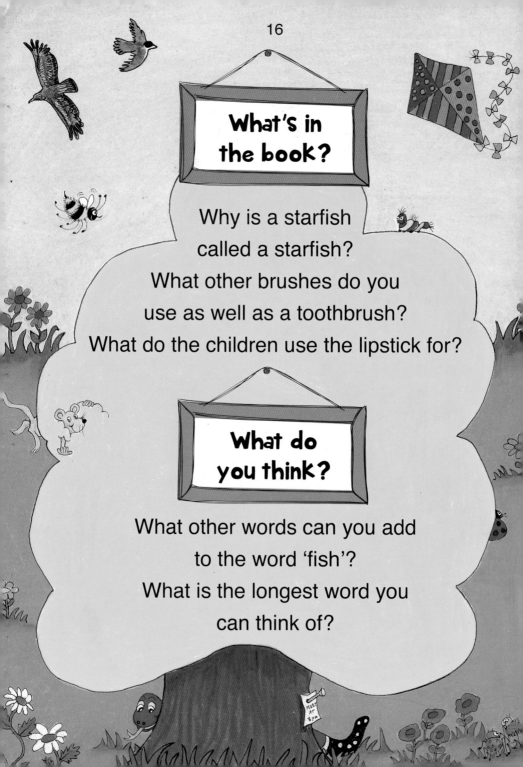

What's in the book?

Why is a starfish
called a starfish?
What other brushes do you
use as well as a toothbrush?
What do the children use the lipstick for?

What do you think?

What other words can you add
to the word 'fish'?
What is the longest word you
can think of?

A Dog Has Pups

I am a dog.

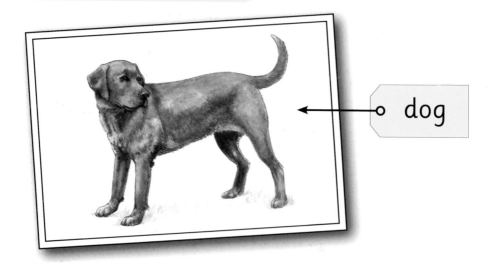

dog

A dog has pups.

pups

I am a goat.

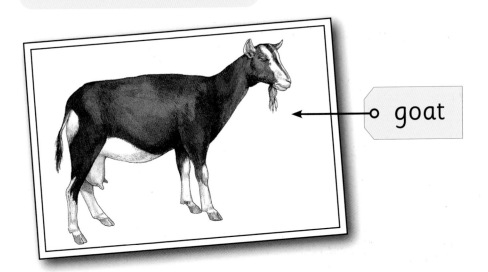

goat

A goat has a kid.

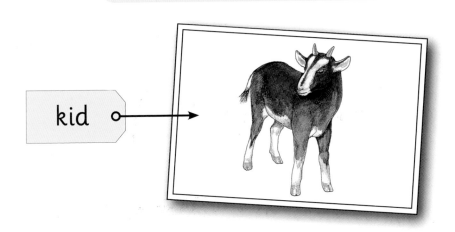

kid

I am a horse.

horse

foal

A horse has a foal.

I am a sheep.

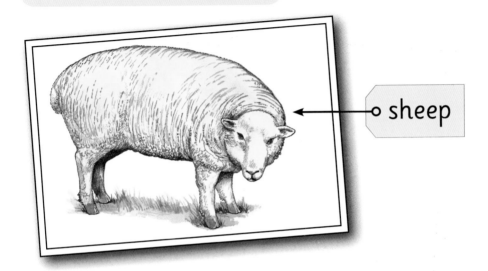

sheep

A sheep has a lamb.

lamb

I am a cat.

cat

kittens

A cat has kittens.

I am a rabbit.

rabbit

A rabbit has kittens too.

kittens

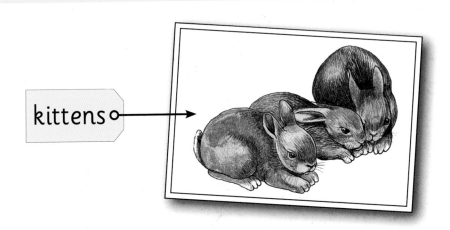

I am a hen.

hen

eggs

A hen has eggs...

hen

eggs

chicks

...that hatch into chicks!

What's in the book?

What is a baby horse called?

A lamb is a baby what?

What are baby rabbits called?

What do you think?

Which animal do you like best?

Can you think of other animals that hatch from eggs?

A Shoal of Fish

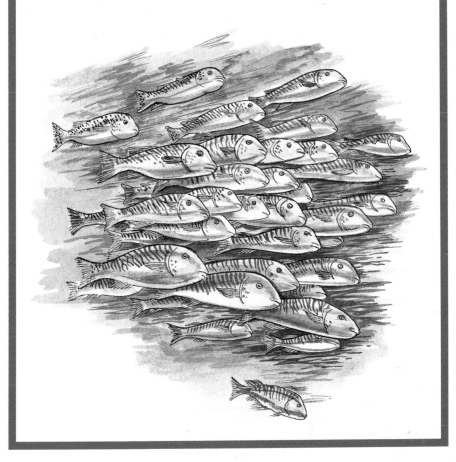

A shoal of fish.

fish

A flock of sheep.

sheep

A herd of goats.

goats

A pack of dogs.

dogs

A litter of kittens.

kittens

A troop of kangaroos.

kangaroos

A skulk of foxes...

foxes

...and a paddling
of ducks!

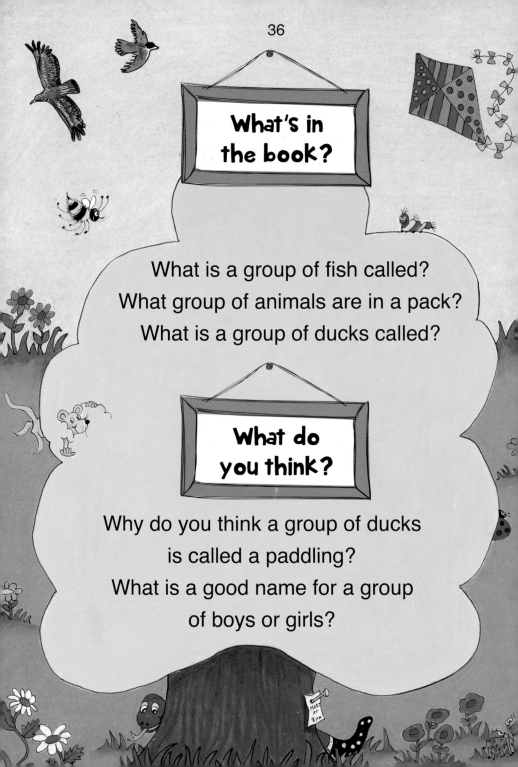

What's in the book?

What is a group of fish called?

What group of animals are in a pack?

What is a group of ducks called?

What do you think?

Why do you think a group of ducks is called a paddling?

What is a good name for a group of boys or girls?

Slugs and Snails

Slugs and snails.

snails

slugs

Snails have shells.

shell

Slugs do not have shells.

As a snail gets bigger,
its shell gets bigger too.

eggs

Slugs and snails hatch from eggs.

Slugs and snails live under things...

rock

...in the damp and dark.

pot

trail

This snail has left a silver trail on the ground.

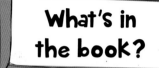

What's in the book?

Do snails have shells?
What do slugs and snails hatch from?
What do slugs and snails leave
on the ground behind them?

What do you think?

Why do slugs and snails like the dark?
Would you like to carry your home
around with you?

FoxeS

Foxes

This is a dog fox.

dog fox

This is a vixen.

vixen

This vixen has three cubs.

cubs

brush

A fox's tail is a brush.

Foxes live in dens.

den

Foxes dig dens under the ground.

Foxes hunt in the dark.

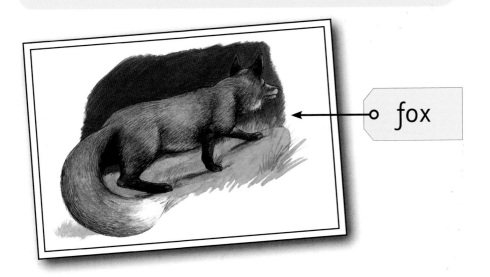

fox

Look out,
rabbit!

rabbit

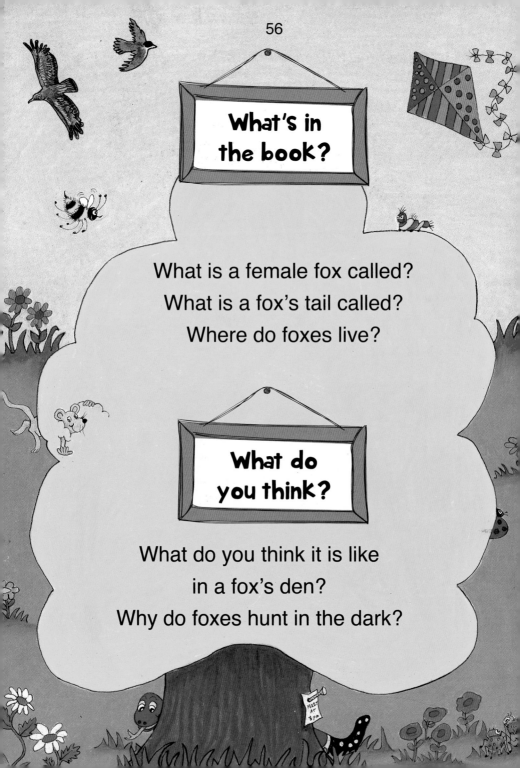

What's in the book?

What is a female fox called?

What is a fox's tail called?

Where do foxes live?

What do you think?

What do you think it is like
in a fox's den?

Why do foxes hunt in the dark?

Insects

An insect has six legs.

It has a hard skin.

Insects can shed this
skin to get bigger.

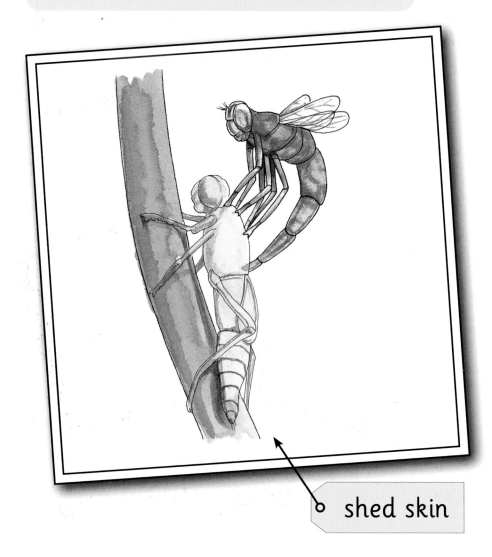

shed skin

Lots of insects have wings.

Insects hatch from eggs...

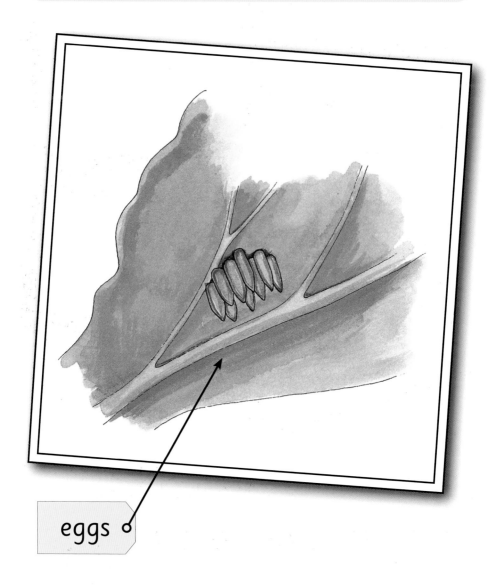

eggs

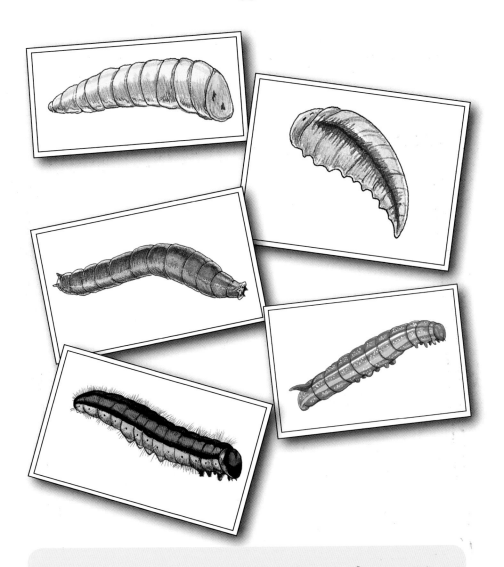

...and start as grubs,
maggots or caterpillars.

Born as caterpillars...

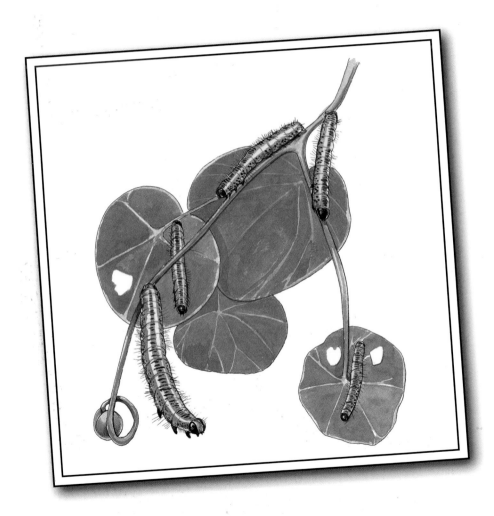

...end as butterflies!

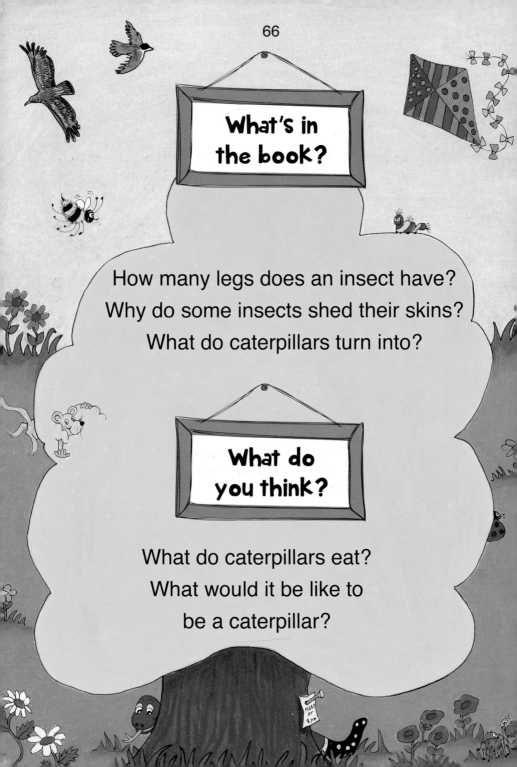

What's in the book?

How many legs does an insect have?
Why do some insects shed their skins?
What do caterpillars turn into?

What do you think?

What do caterpillars eat?
What would it be like to
be a caterpillar?

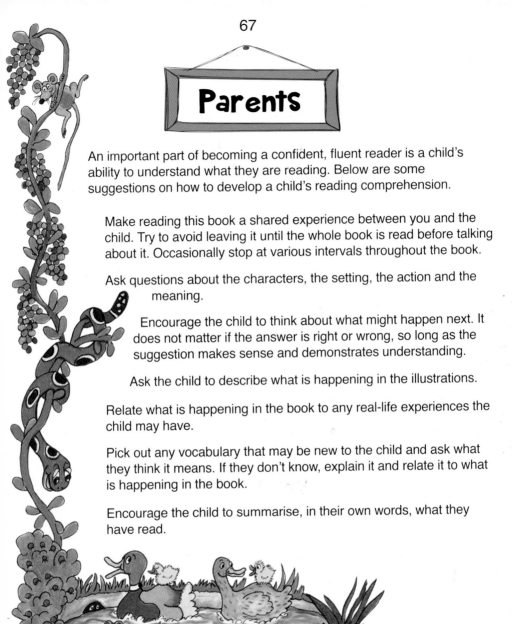

Parents

An important part of becoming a confident, fluent reader is a child's ability to understand what they are reading. Below are some suggestions on how to develop a child's reading comprehension.

Make reading this book a shared experience between you and the child. Try to avoid leaving it until the whole book is read before talking about it. Occasionally stop at various intervals throughout the book.

Ask questions about the characters, the setting, the action and the meaning.

Encourage the child to think about what might happen next. It does not matter if the answer is right or wrong, so long as the suggestion makes sense and demonstrates understanding.

Ask the child to describe what is happening in the illustrations.

Relate what is happening in the book to any real-life experiences the child may have.

Pick out any vocabulary that may be new to the child and ask what they think it means. If they don't know, explain it and relate it to what is happening in the book.

Encourage the child to summarise, in their own words, what they have read.

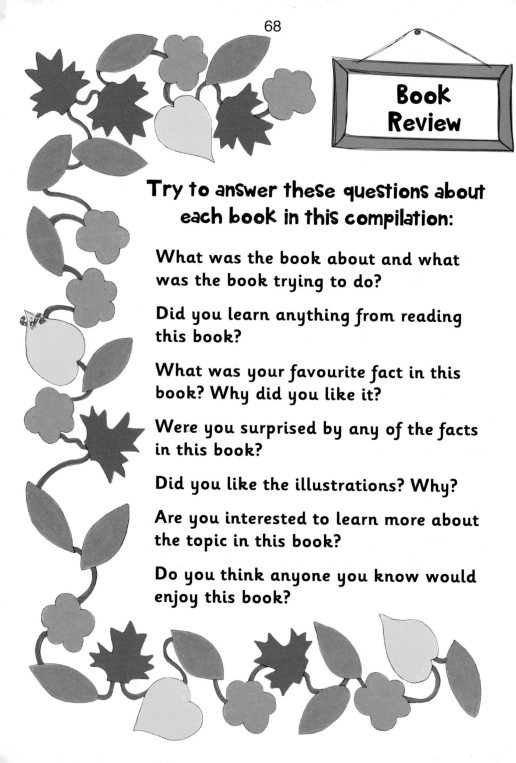

Book Review

Try to answer these questions about each book in this compilation:

What was the book about and what was the book trying to do?

Did you learn anything from reading this book?

What was your favourite fact in this book? Why did you like it?

Were you surprised by any of the facts in this book?

Did you like the illustrations? Why?

Are you interested to learn more about the topic in this book?

Do you think anyone you know would enjoy this book?

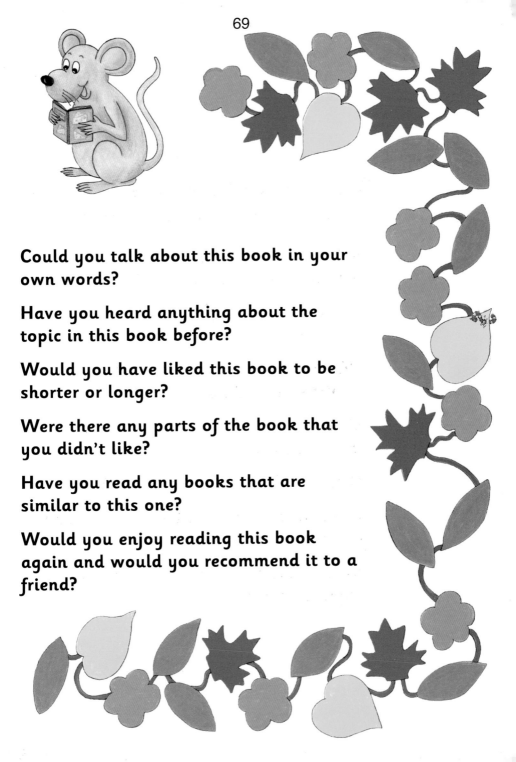

Could you talk about this book in your own words?

Have you heard anything about the topic in this book before?

Would you have liked this book to be shorter or longer?

Were there any parts of the book that you didn't like?

Have you read any books that are similar to this one?

Would you enjoy reading this book again and would you recommend it to a friend?

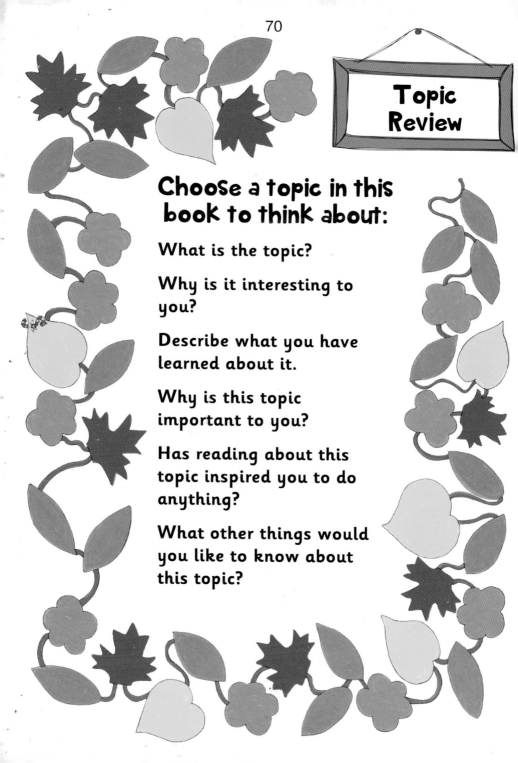

Topic Review

Choose a topic in this book to think about:

What is the topic?

Why is it interesting to you?

Describe what you have learned about it.

Why is this topic important to you?

Has reading about this topic inspired you to do anything?

What other things would you like to know about this topic?